My Earth & Space Science Library

Changes on Earth

Lisa J. Amstutz

Rourke
Educational Media

A Division of
Carson Dellosa Education

ROURKE'S
SCHOOL to HOME
CONNECTIONS
BEFORE AND DURING READING ACTIVITIES

Before Reading: *Building Background Knowledge and Vocabulary*

Building background knowledge can help children process new information and build upon what they already know. Before reading a book, it is important to tap into what children already know about the topic. This will help them develop their vocabulary and increase their reading comprehension.

Questions and Activities to Build Background Knowledge:

1. Look at the front cover of the book and read the title. What do you think this book will be about?
2. What do you already know about this topic?
3. Take a book walk and skim the pages. Look at the table of contents, photographs, captions, and bold words. Did these text features give you any information or predictions about what you will read in this book?

Vocabulary: *Vocabulary Is Key to Reading Comprehension*

Use the following directions to prompt a conversation about each word.
- Read the vocabulary words.
- What comes to mind when you see each word?
- What do you think each word means?

Vocabulary Words:
- *crust*
- *erosion*
- *landslide*
- *shore*

During Reading: *Reading for Meaning and Understanding*

To achieve deep comprehension of a book, children are encouraged to use close reading strategies. During reading, it is important to have children stop and make connections. These connections result in deeper analysis and understanding of a book.

 Close Reading a Text

During reading, have children stop and talk about the following:
- Any confusing parts
- Any unknown words
- Text to text, text to self, text to world connections
- The main idea in each chapter or heading

Encourage children to use context clues to determine the meaning of any unknown words. These strategies will help children learn to analyze the text more thoroughly as they read.

When you are finished reading this book, turn to the last page for an **After Reading Activity**.

Table of Contents

Earth Is Changing 4

Fast Changes 6

Slow Changes 14

Photo Glossary 22

Activity 23

Index 24

After Reading Activity 24

About the Author 24

Earth Is Changing

Mountains rise. Rivers flow.

Earth's surface is always changing!

The path of this river flows around land.

Fast Changes

Changes can happen quickly.

Earthquakes split the Earth's **crust**.

Volcanoes spew lava. When lava cools, new rock forms.

Whoosh! Rocks crash to the ground.
A **landslide** changes the side
of a mountain.

Huge waves crash.

Waves during a storm can reshape the ocean's **shore**.

Floods wash away rock and soil.

They can change the path of a river.

Slow Changes

Other changes happen slowly.
They take many years.

The Grand Canyon was formed over millions of years.

Wind, water, and ice slowly break down rocks.

This is called **erosion**.

Erosion can make canyons. A canyon is a low place with steep sides all around.

Wind erosion helped shape this canyon.

The Earth's crust moves. Parts of it push together. This can form mountains.

19

A fault is a crack in Earth's crust. Faults can be skinny or wide.

Earth is changing every day!

Faults are found on land and under water.

crust (kruhst): The hard outer layer of a planet.

erosion (i-ROH-zhuhn): The gradual wearing away of a substance by water or wind, as in soil erosion.

landslide (LAND-slide): A mass of dirt and rocks that suddenly slides down a mountain or hill.

shore (shor): The land along the edge of an ocean, a river, or a lake.

Erosion Experiment

Try this activity to find out how fast different materials erode.

Supplies

4 trays (plastic or metal)   clay

sand   watering can

gravel   water

soil

Directions

1. Fill each tray with a different material. Prop up one end of the tray.

2. Use a watering can to pour water over each tray.

3. Watch what happens as the water flows. Which material erodes the fastest?

23

Index

change(s) 6, 8, 12, 14
Earth('s) 4, 6, 18, 20
earthquakes 6
mountain(s) 4, 8, 18
river(s) 4, 5, 12
rock(s) 7, 8, 12, 16

About the Author

Lisa J. Amstutz is the author of more than 100 children's books. She loves learning about science and sharing fun facts with kids. Lisa lives on a small farm with her family, two goats, a flock of chickens, and a dog named Daisy.

After Reading Activity

Use a candy bar to build your understanding of Earth's shifting plates. Choose a candy bar with multiple layers. Using a fork, make a crack in the chocolate. This is like a fault in the Earth's crust. Next, pull the candy bar apart. Then, push it together. This shows how mountains form from plates pushing together. Finally, eat your Earth crust candy bar!

Library of Congress PCN Data

Changes on Earth / Lisa J. Amstutz
(My Earth and Space Science Library)
ISBN (hard cover)(alk. paper) 978-1-73163-843-4
ISBN (soft cover) 978-1-73163-920-2
ISBN (e-Book) 978-1-73163-997-4
ISBN (e-Pub) 978-1-73164-074-1
Library of Congress Control Number: 2020930249

Rourke Educational Media
Printed in the United States of America
01-1942011937

www.rourkeeducationalmedia.com

Edited by: Hailey Scragg
Cover design by: Rhea Magaro-Wallace
Interior design by: Jen Bowers
Photo Credits: Cover logo: frog © Eric Phol, test tube © Sergey Lazarev, p4 © Arseniy Rogov, p5 © nazar_ab, p6 © Alexlky, p7 lava flow © Vershinin–M, lava rock © abadonian, p8 © tirc83, p9 © gece33, p10 © ShannonStent, p12 © 2018 Nancy Nehring, p13 © Gibson Outdoor Photography, LLC, p14 © Agnieszka Gaul, p16 © foto Voyager, p18 © AndrewSoundarajan, p20 © Elsvander Gun, p21 © Lindsay Lou, p22 shore © adamkaz, All interior images from istockphoto.com.